GREAT DEBATES
TOUGH QUESTIONS / SMART HISTORY

CHURCH & STATE

By
Geoffrey C. Harrison
and
Thomas F. Scott

NORWOODHOUSE PRESS
CHICAGO, ILLINOIS

Norwood House Press
PO Box 316598
Chicago, Illinois 60631

For information regarding Norwood House Press, please visit our website at:
www.norwoodhousepress.com or call 866-565-2900.

Photo Credits:
Library of Congress (4, 9, 10, 12, 16, 17, 18, 23, 24, 35, 36, 43, 44);
Associated Press (21, 27, 30, 33, 38); Black Book Partners (29); Getty Images (40).

Cover Photos: Jim Beckel/AP (left), Sandy Huffaker/Corbis/Corbis /APImages.

Edited by Mark Stewart and Mike Kennedy.
Designed by Ron Jaffe.
Special thanks to Content Consultant Kim Greene.

Library of Congress Cataloging-in-Publication Data

Harrison, Geoffrey.
  Church and state / by Geoffrey C. Harrison and Thomas F. Scott ;
edited by
Mark Stewart and Mike Kennedy.
    pages cm. -- (Great debates)
  Includes bibliographical references and index.
  Summary: "Informational text uses a historical framework to discuss
issues surrounding separation of church and state. Sections include
opinions from notable Americans on various sides of the issue followed
by encouragement for readers to analyze each opinion."— Provided by
the publisher.
  ISBN 978-1-59953-589-0 (library edition : alk. paper) --
  ISBN 978-1-60357-569-0 (ebook)
1. Church and state--Juvenile literature. I.
Scott, Thomas F. II. Title.
  BV630.3.H37 2013
  322'.10973--dc23
                                        2013017064

COVER: The separation of church and state has been a crucial
designation since the formation of the United States as a nation.

Contents

INTRODUCTION

Note: Words that are **bolded** in the text are defined in the glossary.

INTRODUCTION

We have issues ...

Histry doesn't just happen. It isn't made simply with the delivery of a speech or the stroke of a pen. If you look closely at every important event in the story of America, you are likely to discover deep thinking, courageous action, powerful emotion ... and great debates.

This book explores the debate over where to draw the line between church and state. Through the great freedoms it offers, America has always tried to be a nation with a common identity and common goals. The ability to worship as one pleases is among the most important of an individual's basic rights. Yet many believe that religion poses the greatest threat to the American way of life because of how it can divide us.

What does "Church and State" mean? Church is a simple way of saying *organized religions*, or *religious leaders*, that hold certain sets of beliefs. It does not refer to any one religion or house of worship. State is a simple way of saying

Separation of church and state has been debated for centuries. In this engraving from 1871, religious leaders appeal to Lady Justice, who represents the government.

Join the Debate

Debate is the art of discussing a controversial topic using logic and reason. One side takes the affirmative side of an issue and the other takes the negative side. Remember, however, that a great debate does not necessarily need to be an argument—often it is a matter of opinion, with each side supporting its viewpoint with facts. The key is to gather enough information to create a strong opinion. Out in the real world, debate has fewer rules and can get noisy and ugly. But on the big issues in America, debate is often how compromises are made and things get done.

civil authority, the part of government that enforces laws and keeps order. It does not refer to any particular state or branch of government.

The relationship between church and state in America goes back nearly 400 years. Among the first European settlers were colonists hoping to free themselves from **religious oppression** in Europe. During the 1600s and 1700s, people from several branches of Christianity came to America, where they found freedom, opportunity, and sometimes danger. So, too, did small groups of Jewish people and Muslims. In most places, church and state worked hand-in-hand as a matter of safety and survival. Many colonies had official religions, and non-members were prevented by law from holding elected office. By the mid-1700s, Americans could be described as being very religious people.

Make Your Case

In Chapter 2 through Chapter 5, you will find special sections entitled **Make Your Case**. Each one highlights different sides of the debate on separation of church and state using quotes from prominent Americans. **Make Your Case** lets you analyze the speaker's point of view ... and challenges you to form an opinion of your own. You'll find additional famous opinion-makers on the debate in Chapter 7.

Revolution broke out in 1776, and the colonists went to war with England to gain their independence. The new nation's government didn't choose an official religion (as England had) but instead specifically chose no religion at all. The founding fathers decided that their new experiment in democracy needed to be free of religious interference. Both church and state would be stronger, they believed, if neither meddled in the other's affairs.

The founding fathers next turned their attention to mapping out the political future of the United States. On the topic of religion, they were crystal clear. Their goal was to limit its influence in government. They believed that the business of government was governing, and that matters of religion should be left to the different churches. Keep this in mind as you read about these great debates.

1

Does religious freedom create a stronger society?

America's most influential writer in the late 1700s was Thomas Paine. He had a way of making complex ideas easy for everyone to understand, even those who could not read. Paine felt that religious faith should exist between an individual and God. He thought that large, organized religions were too interested in gaining power and money. Of course, not all of the new nation's leaders agreed. When it came time to write the Constitution and Bill of Rights, the influence of religion in matters of government became a subject of intense debate ...

AFFIRMATIVE SIDE

America survived and grew because of the partnership between religion and government. Why ruin a good thing? Imagine how strong this country can be if the values of the church are shared by the state, and the values of the state are shared by the church!

Thomas Paine was one of the first political figures to shape opinion on church and state.

Thinking Independently

Many influential leaders shared the views of Paine. That was apparent when the Declaration of Independence was written in 1776. The word "God" appeared only once, and not in a way that promoted any religious ideas. This was a significant departure from official documents of European countries, which typically made reference to "Christianity" or "The Lord" or "Jesus." Something else caught the eye of many people. The term "Laws of Nature" was included in the Declaration of Independence, and it was capitalized. This was a signal that Americans considered freedom a human right, not a religious one.

NEGATIVE SIDE

History has taught us a valuable lesson: The more involved religion and government are, the more corruption and bloodshed are likely to exist. America has a clean slate. Let's build a country where religions can flourish without government meddling, and where laws are made for people of all faiths.

"Let us with caution indulge the **supposition** that morality can be maintained without religion."

▶ *George Washington, 1796*

In Washington's farewell address as president, he questioned whether America could stay on course without involving religion—or at least religious principles—in government.

How might Americans in the 1790s have responded to Washington's idea?

The authors of the Declaration of Independence did not deny the existence of God. In fact, they thought of God as a supreme being who created the world and the laws of nature. Many considered themselves Deists. Deists believed in God. However, they did not accept the notion that God delivered knowledge to people, that God was the source of all religious knowledge, or that the miracles described in the Bible were real. Deists thought that life followed the laws of nature, not the laws of any one religion. The laws of nature, they said, were enough to prove the existence of God.

Deism began in the late 1600s and was popular among the educated upper classes in America and Europe. It appealed to those who had a thirst for scientific knowledge. Thomas Jefferson probably counted himself as a Deist. That would explain some of the wording in the Declaration of Independence. In his original draft, Jefferson made a reference to Christianity in a very negative way. It was edited out of the final version.

Many believe that Benjamin Franklin and James Madison, along with other founding fathers, thought of themselves as Deists. This belief system remained popular until the early 1800s, but it was very much in play when the nation's key documents were being written. Later, many Deists gravitated toward the Unitarian branch of Christianity, which embraced many of their basic ideas.

A Framework for Governing

After the Revolutionary War, when the founding fathers began writing the Constitution, they were careful to exclude religion from official matters. For example, elected or appointed officials no longer had to pass "religious

"The purpose of separation of church and state is to keep forever from these shores the ceaseless strife that has soaked the soil of Europe in blood for centuries."

▶ *James Madison, 1803*

Madison is said to have written these words in a letter that has long since disappeared. Like many of the founding fathers, he believed a major benefit of the separation of church and state would mean an end to large-scale religious violence.

Does having no "official" religion keep a country from suffering through religious wars?

tests." This had not been the case in colonial America. Also, when being sworn in, the word "God" was not a part of the President's official oath.

The Constitution mostly covered what the government could and could not do. The Bill of Rights added **amendments** to the Constitution. These addressed the rights of United States citizens. In the First Amendment, Congress was prohibited from making a law that prevented the establishment of a religion or kept people from worshiping in whatever way they wanted.

In the years that followed, many of the founding fathers wrote about or discussed the separation of church and state.

They were aware that important Christian groups wanted a society similar to colonial times, when the churches held more power. Political leaders such as Jefferson, Madison, and Franklin made the point again and again that mixing government and organized religion would damage both. In a letter written in 1802, Jefferson talked about a "wall of separation between church and state." This was actually the first time the phrase "church and state" appeared in any kind of document.

Now consider *this* ...

America's unique position in the world as a government without a **state religion** came into play in the 1790s. During this era, Barbary Pirates based in North Africa presented a constant threat to shipping in the Mediterranean. Hoping to avoid war, the U.S. signed the Treaty of Tripoli. In it was a section that made it clear that America was not a "Christian nation" and that it respected the Muslim religion of the **Ottoman government**. Today, America is viewed by some people in the Islamic faith as a threat—despite the fact that it still has no official religion, and millions of Muslims enjoy the rights and freedoms of American citizenship. **Why might some Muslims feel threatened by a country with no official religion?**

2 Should there be limits to religious freedom in our society?

The founding fathers thought it was important that the Constitution protect all religious beliefs and practices. But when they approved the First Amendment, they may not have expected that it would deal with belief systems that strayed far from Christianity. By the same token, it was also understood that any religious belief or practice that violated the rights of another person—or that broke a law—would be covered by other parts of the Bill of Rights. By the mid-1800s, however, some openly challenged this assumption, triggering the first great debate about church and state …

AFFIRMATIVE SIDE

The First Amendment says the United States government cannot make a law "prohibiting the free exercise of religion." Therefore, whatever my religion tells me to do—whatever I understand to be my religious duty—should be protected by the Constitution.

The Mormons

In 1878, the U.S. Supreme Court heard a case that brought up questions about how the Constitution was worded. At the time, the **Mormon** religion believed in polygamy—that its male members could have more than one wife. A federal law passed in 1862 made this a crime. George Reynolds, a high-ranking member of the Mormon church, was married to two women. He decided to test the **constitutionality** of this law.

Reynolds claimed that having more than one wife was his religious duty. In this case, all seven Supreme Court justices agreed that his argument was weak. They made reference to the fact that Thomas Jefferson had actually addressed this point of religious duty when he wrote that religious belief was indeed protected by the Constitution. However, actions that are *encouraged* by religious belief do not necessarily deserve the same protection.

NEGATIVE SIDE

The government needs to apply some common sense in terms of the First Amendment. The Christian crusaders in the 12th and 13th centuries thought it was their religious duty to kill Muslims. This is totally unacceptable in the United States.

THE MORMON PROBLEM SOLVED.

This political cartoon from the 1870s dramatizes the conflicts that could arise between Mormons and the federal government.

At the time, most Americans applauded this decision. They may have felt that the Mormons deserved to worship as they pleased, but this was a case where the "greater good" had to be considered. Clearly, the government and its laws took **precedent** over religious freedom. For instance, what if a religion believed in human sacrifice? Should the Constitution protect that practice? In the end, the court decided that the First Amendment protected the ideas and opinions of a religion, but not the actions of its followers if they broke the law.

Influence of Technology

Debates over the separation of church and state have also been triggered by new trends and technologies. For

Make Your Case

"If religious books are not widely circulated among the masses in this country, I do not know what is going to become of us as a nation."

▶ *Daniel Webster, 1820*

Webster was a leading politician in the first half of the 1800s. He also served as **Secretary of State** and ran for president. Webster was not known as a religious man, but he believed that strong religious beliefs served a positive purpose for the young nation.

Should our government encourage religious values, even if it cannot endorse any one religion?

instance, during the 20th century it became an issue in the movie business. In the early 1900s, Americans discovered an exciting new form of entertainment: motion pictures. In 1915, a film called *The Birth of a Nation* stirred up protests across the country because it showed racist scenes that disturbed many Americans. Many lawsuits followed, and eventually the Supreme Court was asked to

Make Your Case

"They knew that to put God in the Constitution was to put man out."

▶ *Robert Ingersoll, 1883*

Ingersoll was a popular lecturer in the late 1800s. He believed that the founding fathers made a brilliant choice in their wording of the First Amendment. He felt it kept religions from becoming too powerful.

How might an official religion in the U.S. have taken advantage of its power?

weigh in. The court ruled that film companies were businesses and therefore did not enjoy the rights guaranteed by the First Amendment. In this particular case, the issue was freedom of speech.

Based on this decision, many states and cities set up movie censorship boards. Before a film could be shown in a theater, it had to be approved by the local board. If the board members believed it was indecent or offensive, they would not grant the theater owner a license to show the film. If a movie house disregarded its censorship board, the owner could be fined or even jailed. Standards for decency differed wildly from town to town. Films were banned for all sorts of reasons. Some boards objected to scenes that showed children of different races playing together. Others banned movies that dealt with subjects such as pregnancy.

Now consider *this* ...

In 1952, a film called *The Miracle* was banned by censors in New York City. Cardinal Francis Spellman—the leader of the city's Catholic church—announced that the movie was **sacrilegious** and convinced the board to prevent it from being shown. The company behind the film sued because the decision was made on religious grounds. Once again, it was a freedom of speech issue, but it also involved the separation of church and state. This time, the Supreme Court found that, although it was still a business, the film industry had become an important means for communicating ideas—so it could not be censored in this way anymore. **Why is it important for the Supreme Court to be able to "change its mind" as the times change?**

Does the church-and-state debate belong in the classroom?

The separation of church and state in schools did not attract much attention until about 100 years ago. Many public schools began the day with a prayer or a reading from the Bible. However, a growing movement to remove religious viewpoints from the classroom gained strength in 1925, when a Tennessee educator named John Scopes was found guilty of breaking a state law after discussing evolution in his science class. Soon, more and more attention was focused on religious instruction in public schools and the behavior of school boards. This led to another important debate …

AFFIRMATIVE SIDE

The basic values of American education are the same as the basic values of every major religion. Promoting religion in public schools is not the goal; promoting those values is. There is no reason to make public schools "religion-free" zones.

For many years, public school students across the country started their day with a prayer.

Bus Stop

In 1947, the Supreme Court heard a case about a school board in New Jersey that had refunded bus fare to parents of children attending a local Catholic school. The children received religious training at their school, and the money came from tax dollars paid to the local government. In a close decision, the court ruled that reimbursing bus fare did not go against the Constitution. The justices pointed out that the town policy was to refund bus fare to all families, so no religion had been favored.

NEGATIVE SIDE

The government runs public schools, and therefore they must pass the test of the First Amendment. The government cannot use its power to promote any religion. If we break down the barrier between church and state for our children, they may not understand its purpose or importance when they grow up.

"I think that the public school classroom is no place for me to try and impose my world formula for prayer on children who don't share it, and for that very reason, I don't want my children in a public school classroom to be exposed to someone else's religion or formula."

▶ *Philip Hart, 1962*

Hart was a Michigan Senator and a devout Catholic who opposed school prayer. He made these remarks after the Supreme Court decided the landmark case that declared school prayer to be unconstitutional.

In what ways might Hart's remarks have influenced Catholic voters the next time he was up for election?

In its decision, the Supreme Court actually spent more time clarifying the part of the Constitution that says no law can be created that favors one religion over another. The justices reinforced the idea that no law could force someone to go to a church or make someone state a belief in a religion. To underscore their point, they quoted the words of Thomas Jefferson, whose goal was to "erect a wall between Church and State." The debate may have started over bus fare, but the reasoning behind the Supreme Court's decision had a far greater impact.

This case prompted a major turn of events in the United States. It came at a time when many Americans were

President Eisenhower (standing) wanted to add "under God" to the Pledge of Allegiance. Many believed this was a reaction to Communism—which discouraged organized religion—and not a push for "more religion" in the U.S.

looking for ways to strengthen their faith, because of the threat of Communism and the possibility of nuclear war. For instance, in 1954 at the request of President Dwight Eisenhower, the Pledge of Allegiance was changed to include the words "under God." Prior to that, the pledge contained no religious language.

School Prayer

Soon the role of religion in American schools became a topic of debate. Private schools were free to decide how worship and prayer fit into their daily schedules. However, public schools were subject to the rules separating church and state. Did Eisenhower's new Pledge of Allegiance mean that religion was gaining a foothold in these institutions?

Make Your Case

"Eighty percent of the American people want Bible readings and prayer in the schools ... Why should the majority be so severely punished by the protests of a handful?"

▶ *Billy Graham, circa 1980*

America is one of the most religious countries among developed nations. However, the Constitution was written to prevent the majority from getting its way on important legal issues.

Is Graham's view that the majority is "punished" by the First Amendment a fair one?

Some groups believed religion should be kept out of public schools altogether. They pointed out that the First Amendment said that government could not make a law respecting the establishment of a religion. In 1962, the Supreme Court heard a case about voluntary prayer in New York schools. The justices ruled this unconstitutional. The fact that it was voluntary didn't matter. Nor did the fact that it was **non-denominational**.

Did this mean that all religious discussion was no longer allowed in public schools? Not necessarily. In 1971, the Supreme Court made it clear that religious ideas could be taught in schools, as long as they had a non-religious educational purpose. Also, they could not be used to support or oppose a specific religion. In their decision, the justices were careful to point out that separation of church and state could never be total separation—that was impossible. There would always be some involvement of the government in religion, and vice versa. What Jefferson had called a "wall" now looked more like a blurry line.

Now consider *this* ...

In recent years, the debate about religion in public schools has focused on attempts to reintroduce religious beliefs into certain classes for the sake of "balance." For example, Louisiana passed a state law instructing its science teachers to give **Creationism** an equal amount of teaching time to evolution. Creationists do not agree with the scientific theory that life evolved slowly over billions of years. The Supreme Court struck down the Louisiana law on the grounds that it did not improve the way science was being taught in schools, and because it pushed the beliefs of a specific religion. ***In which classes would it be appropriate to discuss belief systems such as Creationism?***

4 Should the government have power over religion?

Despite the separation of church and state, religion has played a huge role in American politics. Any person campaigning in an election can expect to have his or her faith examined. Politicians often offer their religious views as reasons to vote for them. Almost as often, their opponents use those views against them. Sometimes elected officials will try to insert their religious beliefs into the creation of **legislation**. Even if they fail, they can win the favor of like-minded voters. Using religion for political gain is nothing new, but it does bring up an issue worthy of debate …

AFFIRMATIVE SIDE

It's okay for a candidate to campaign on his or her faith. Elected officials cannot make or change laws covering religion. But since my decisions are tied to my religious beliefs, I believe it's fair to make that an issue so I can pick a candidate who shares my views.

Despite worshipping in Christian churches, Barack Obama was accused of being a "secret Muslim."

Playing Politics

When Barack Obama was elected President of the United States in 2008, it was a religious first. Never before had a president (or vice president) been raised in a home that did not follow a Christian religion. In Obama's case, his mother and grandparents encouraged him to explore all faiths, including Islam. As an adult, Obama became a Christian.

During Obama's campaign for president, however, some of his opponents tried to suggest that he was a "secret Muslim." As a child, he had lived for a while in Indonesia, which has the world's largest Muslim population.

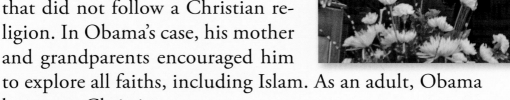

NEGATIVE SIDE

Candidates know that their religious beliefs cannot influence legislation once they are in office. So why is it right to campaign on them? Politicians are being deceitful—and maybe even unconstitutional—when they talk about blurring the line between church and state.

Other opponents looked at Obama's record as a Christian. Some complained that he had not been a regular church-goer, while others thought that the ministers he knew were racist or anti-American.

This type of scrutiny had become commonplace in politics. For more than 150 years, members of the Catholic faith found running for office extremely difficult outside of their home areas. Because Catholics follow the Pope as their spiritual leader, some Americans wondered what would happen if he instructed an elected official to do something that went against the Constitution.

A Question of Faith

Al Smith was the governor of New York in the 1920s. He was also Catholic. Smith was very popular

Make Your Case

"A loyal Roman Catholic if elected to the presidency would be bound to obey the pope, even if it conflicted with his responsibilities to the American people as set forth in the Constitution."

► *James Tolle, 1960*

Tolle was a Christian activist who believed that there could be no separation of church and state if John F. Kennedy, a Catholic, were to be elected president.

How might the American public have reacted had Kennedy gone against American interests on instructions from the Pope?

Make Your Case

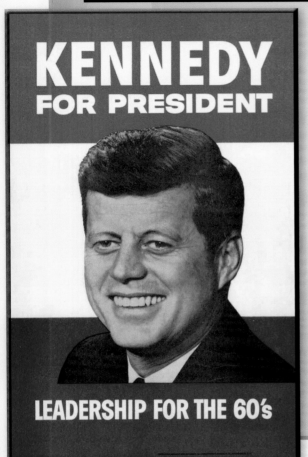

KENNEDY
FOR PRESIDENT

LEADERSHIP FOR THE 60's

"Whatever one's religion in private life may be, for the office-holder, nothing takes precedence over his oath to uphold the Constitution and all its parts—including the First Amendment and the strict separation of church and state."

► *John F. Kennedy, 1959*

Kennedy was a presidential candidate when he said these words. Clearly, he knew that his religion would be an issue in the election.

Should a politician's religious beliefs come into play during an election?

for improving the way government was run and how it helped people in need. Smith ran for president in 1928 but lost the election. Voters were not convinced that he would put his office above his faith.

By 1960, views on Catholicism had changed enough so that John F. Kennedy won a narrow presidential victory. Forty years later, Al Gore selected Joe Lieberman as his

When Keith Ellison was elected to the Senate in 2006, he used the Qu'ran when being sworn in.

vice-presidential candidate when running for president. The pair lost one of the closest elections in history. Lieberman would have been the first person of Jewish faith to hold such a high office. Some believe his religion may have played a role in the loss at the polls.

In 2006, Keith Ellison ran for U.S. Congress in Minnesota. A practicing Muslim, he won the election and became the first person of his faith to go to Washington.

Ellison posed for his official swearing-in photo with his hand on the **Qu'ran** instead of the Bible. Some people complained about this choice. Ellison pointed out that the Qu'ran used for the photo had originally been owned by Thomas Jefferson!

Attacking candidates for their religious beliefs is nothing new, of course. Jefferson faced defeat in the presidential election of 1797 because of claims he was anti-Christian. His opponents pointed to his involvement in writing the Constitution!

Now consider *this* ...

Religious institutions in the U.S. do not have to pay taxes on the money they earn. This is an important part of the separation of church and state. At the same time, religious institutions are prohibited from endorsing political candidates, which is equally important. Even so, throughout history, different religious groups have usually favored one political party over another. Members of a certain religion tend to vote together for candidates whose religious beliefs—or whose policies—mirror their own. For example, during much of the 20th century, Catholics favored the Democratic party because it was seen as protecting the rights of everyday workers. *If religions in America could officially endorse candidates, how might this change the nature of political campaigns?*

Is there room for God in government policy?

The United States has the world's largest Christian population. But in following their religious beliefs, some public officials overstep their authority. In 2002, a law requiring schools to begin each day with a patriotic oath was passed in Elk Grove, California. The legislation also said that no child could be forced to participate. One elementary school settled on the Pledge of Allegiance, even though it includes a reference to God. This led to a debate that had as much to do with the pledge's wording as its religious message ...

AFFIRMATIVE SIDE

The Pledge of Allegiance asks people to be true to the flag and the values that it symbolizes, including liberty and justice for everyone. You are free to refuse to recite the pledge, but it's un-American to prevent others from taking this oath. It does not ask people to swear their faith to God.

A protestor in Elk Grove points out that the original Pledge of Allegiance did not include a reference to God.

One Nation Under God?

The law in Elk Grove created an issue for atheists. Atheism does not accept any religion that worships God or any other supernatural power. The father of a child in Elk Grove said that his daughter was harmed when her

NEGATIVE SIDE

The word God automatically makes the Pledge of Allegiance a religious oath, and therefore it is unconstitutional to recite it in public schools. It doesn't matter what religion you follow. The pledge specifically references religion, and the First Amendment says this is unconstitutional.

schoolmates recited the Pledge of Allegiance because of his family's atheist beliefs. He argued that the phrase "one nation under God" made the young girl feel that she was not part of the nation to which her friends and teachers were pledging their allegiance every day.

The Supreme Court agreed. The justices looked at the history of the Pledge of Allegiance, which did not include any mention of God when it became the nation's official oath of loyalty in 1893. They noted that those words were inserted 51 years later for a specific "religious" purpose. Therefore, Elk Grove's policy to use the Pledge of Allegiance was deemed unconstitutional.

Quiet Time

Another controversial topic related to religion in public schools is the idea of silent meditation. What used to be called "quiet time" was seen as an opportunity by some religious groups to put prayer back into the classroom. After all, if a child is just *thinking* quietly, who's to say what is going on inside his or her head? But problems arose when Alabama changed the rules of quiet time. The state passed legislation saying it was legal for children to practice "voluntary prayer" during this part of the day.

The debate reached the Supreme Court, which struck down the law. The justices agreed there was nothing wrong with starting a day with silent meditation. But adding the voluntary prayer **provision** to the law clearly violated the

"Those who would renegotiate the boundaries between church and state must therefore answer a difficult question: Why would we trade a system that has served us so well for one that has served others so poorly?"

▶ *Sandra Day O'Connor, 1984*

O'Connor was a Supreme Court Justice. She made these remarks after voting that it was unconstitutional to keep framed copies of the Ten Commandments on the walls of two Kentucky courthouses. She was outvoted, and they were allowed to stay.

What might someone visiting the Kentucky courthouses find offensive about the framed Ten Commandments?

court's earlier decision that religion itself could not be promoted or endorsed in public schools.

Other First Amendment debates were not so clear. For example, is it okay for a student to write a prayer for the school football team and read it over the loudspeaker before the game on a Friday night? This question triggered several court cases, which looked at the issue of separation of church and state.

Make Your Case

"If we ever forget that we're one nation under God, then we will be one nation gone under."

▶ *Ronald Reagan, 1984*

Reagan is remembered as a president who encouraged religious viewpoints in the national discussion. However, he said it was important to keep church and state separate.

Should discussions of faith have a place in deciding issues such as the funding of social programs or aid to foreign countries?

It also opened debate on another part of the First Amendment that guarantees free speech. If a student stands up in front of a crowd at a school function and makes a speech reflecting his religious beliefs, his words are considered free speech and protected by the Constitution. However, if a public school gives that same student a microphone so he or she can make the same statement over the school's loudspeaker system, his words run afoul of the Constitution.

Now consider *this* ...

The Supreme Court rulings on cases that concern the separation of church and state bother many Americans who fully support the ideas put forth in the Constitution and Bill of Rights. They worry that endless legal arguments will squash the spirit of these important documents, and in doing so alter the original vision of the role of religion in the United States. For example, one day you may go to a sporting event and find out that it is no longer legal for the crowd to sing *God Bless America* because it contains religious messages that may offend people in the crowd. Our national anthem—*The Star-Spangled Banner*—contains a religious message in the third verse. It is entirely possible that the Supreme Court could one day be asked to brand this song unconstitutional. **If this happened, would it be right to remove the word "God" and keep the song as our national anthem?**

6 Find your voice

The debate over same-sex marriage has become a major issue for some in the separation of church and state.

I n recent years, three issues have been at the center of the debate on separation of church and state. These are complicated questions that invite many points of view. Much like other issues in this debate, they involve economics, politics, powerful fears, and strong emotions. There is a very good chance that people will be debating these issues throughout your lifetime.

1

Can the government prevent two men or two women from getting married?

Same-sex marriage has become a hotly debated topic in recent years. Those who oppose it on religious grounds offer several arguments. They say that it defeats the traditional reason for getting married: to have children. They also say that it is immoral or against God's will. They fear that same-sex marriage will encourage people to seek out same-sex relationships. Some have made the point that it violates their First Amendment right to worship freely, because legalizing same-sex marriage on the federal level might mean their religion would be "forced" by law to accept same-sex couples.

Supporters of same-sex marriage do not accept any of these arguments. They claim that same-sex marriage is a **civil right**. It enables same-sex couples to share in benefits that "traditional" husbands and wives now enjoy, including health insurance, tax status, and legal privileges. To those who would use religious documents such as the Bible to outlaw same-sex marriage, supporters point out that society has moved past a lot of ideas contained in these works. It's time to move past this one, too.

2

Should the government fund scientists who are doing stem cell research?

Stem cells are special cells that can transform into whatever the body needs. The medical world believes that they hold great promise for the treatment of diseases, from **Alzheimer's** to different types of cancer, and possibly even for **traumatic injury**. Someday a person could lose a leg in an accident and, with the aid of stem cells, simply grow a "new" one. The problem is that stem cells often come from **embryos** that are created in a lab environment and then terminated. Many religions believe that a human life has already begun at this point. So some people call stem cell research a form of murder. Most scientists disagree. They tend to think that human life starts when the heart begins to beat (at 5 weeks) or when brain activity develops (at 7 or 8 weeks). In order to avoid this controversy, some scientists have looked for other ways to get stem cells. However, it is likely that there will always be a need for embryonic stem cells.

Stem cell research has entered the debate over separation of church and state.

3

The government protects people who want to live as they please. Shouldn't it allow people to die as they please?

As America's population ages and medical expenses soar, "end-of-life" issues have become an important part of the national discussion. It has been said that, for the average person in this country, 90 percent of medical bills come in the final 90 days of life. Often, those days are filled with pain and agony. If a person wishes a peaceful, pain-free death, should doctors help? Or should they use all of their training and technology to keep patients alive as long as possible—even if it's against their wishes? Every religion approaches this question differently. The government has been unclear on the rules for ending a patient's suffering "early"—is it a humane act, or is it murder? Most doctors are unwilling to find out. If the government does pass a federal law covering end-of-life situations, you can bet it will trigger a passionate church-and-state debate!

All the issues in this chapter are being discussed as part of the national debate on church and state. Will we ever reach a "middle ground" on these questions? Now is the time to join the national conversation. Think about these issues and consider both sides of these debates. Where do you stand? One day soon—through the candidates you support, the dollars you spend, and your own personal feelings about church and state—you will have a voice!

7 Point — Counterpoint

The debate on the separation of church and state has been greatly influenced by public opinion over the years. That opinion is shaped by many factors, including personal experience, common sense, and what others write or have to say. We think about the different sides of an issue. We look at how it affects us, our family members, and our friends. We consider the best solutions. And we weigh what the smartest and most influential people believe.

This was true in the 1700s and 1800s, when Americans got their information from pamphlets, newspapers, and speeches. It was true in the 1900s, when radio and television brought ideas to an even wider audience. It remains true today, as we scan websites, blogs, and social media. The voices in this chapter have helped shape the debate on separation of church and state. The words may be a little different, but the passion behind them would fit in any era ...

Point — Counterpoint

"A Turk, a Jew, a Roman Catholic, and what is worse than all, a Universalist, may be President of the United States."

Anonymous letter to the New York Daily Advertiser, 1787 ◀

"Lighthouses are more useful than churches."
▶ *Benjamin Franklin (with walking stick), 1757*

These two quotes show that attitudes toward the church in America during the 1700s differed dramatically. The first demonstrates how dismayed people were to discover that the new nation's leader could be something other than a Christian. The writer was especially alarmed about Universalism, a faith that many at the time thought of as "Godless." Franklin's remark had a couple of meanings. He had actually been shipwrecked several years earlier. Franklin's words were a humorous way of saying that he felt lighthouses saved more souls than religion did.

How might Franklin's dim view of religion have swayed others when it came time to approve the Constitution and the Bill of Rights?

Point — Counterpoint

"They are conducting a **craven** crusade of religious prejudice against Catholic children."
Francis Spellman, 1949 ◄

"Anyone who knows history will recognize that the domination of education or of government by any one particular religious faith is never a happy arrangement for the people."
► *Eleanor Roosevelt (right), 1949*

Cardinal Spellman, the Archbishop of New York, was criticizing supporters of a bill that prohibited public education funds to be used for non-public schools, including Catholic schools. Roosevelt, who was First Lady from 1932 to 1945, disputed the Cardinal's opinion in a magazine column she wrote. She was a firm believer in the separation of church and state. Their war of words became very heated, despite the fact that Spellman and President Franklin Roosevelt had been good friends. The church and state debate had not drawn much attention in the first half of the 20th century, but it made the front pages in the 1940s. *Is withholding tax dollars from schools that teach a specific religion a form of prejudice?*

"Today courts wrongly interpret separation of church and state to mean that religion has no place in the public arena."
Dinesh D'Souza, 2007 ◀

"How dismal it is to see present day Americans yearning for the very **orthodoxy** that their country was founded to escape." ▶ *Christopher Hitchens, 2007*

D'Souza and Hitchens are writers who were born outside the U.S. Social media allows them to reach a wide audience. D'Souza thought that religion should influence the way the country is run. Hitchens found it troubling that many Americans overlook the importance the founding fathers placed on separation of church and state.

How well has the position of the founding fathers on church and state held up since the 1700s?

There has never been a better time to make your voice heard. No matter which side of an issue you take, remember that a debate doesn't have to be an argument. If you enjoy proving your point, join your school's debate team. If your school doesn't have one, find a teacher who will serve as coach and get more students involved. If you want to make a real splash, email the people who represent you in government. If they don't listen now, they may hear from you later … in the voting booth!

GLOSSARY

Alzheimer's — A disease that slowly destroys brain function and memory.

Amendments — Additions to the Constitution.

Civil Right — A right to freedom and equality.

Constitutionality — The state of being in accordance with the Constitution.

Craven — Lacking in courage.

Creationism — The belief that everything in the universe was created by a divine act.

Embryos — Organisms in an early stage of development.

Legislation — A law or group of laws.

Mormon — A religion established in the U.S. in the 1800s. It's also called Church of Jesus Christ of Latter-Day Saints.

Non-Denominational — Not part of any specific religion.

Orthodoxy — A set of generally accepted religious ideas.

Ottoman Government — The controlling organization of the Turkish empire that stretched from the Middle East across North Africa.

Precedent — An earlier action that could serve as an example for future action.

Provision — A condition in a legal document.

Qu'ran — The Islamic sacred book.

Religious Institutions — Churches or organized religions.

Religious Oppression — Unjust treatment based on a person's religion.

Sacrilegious — Violating an idea that is considered sacred.

Same-Sex Marriage — The legal union of two men or two women.

Secretary of State — The head of the department concerned with America's foreign affairs.

State Religion — A country's official religion.

Supposition — An uncertain belief.

Traumatic Injury — An injury that severely damages or destroys part of the body.

SOURCES

The authors relied on many different sources for their information. Listed below are some of their primary sources:

Faith of Our Fathers: Religion and the New Nation. Edwin S. Gaustad. Harper & Row, San Francisco, California, 1987.

Religion and Politics in the United States. Kenneth D. Wald. CQ Press, Washington DC, 1992.

Sacred Causes: The clash of religion and politics, from the Great War to the War on Terror. Michael Burleigh. HarperCollins, New York, 2007.

To Begin the World Anew. Bernard Bailyn. Alfred A. Knopf, New York, 2003.

RESOURCES

For more information on the subjects covered in this book, consider starting with these books and websites:

Encyclopedia of Religion in America. Charles H. Lippy & Peter W. Williams. CQ Press, Washington DC, 2010.

Americans United for Separation of Church and State
www.au.org

Constitution.net
www.usconstitution.net

INDEX

Page numbers in **bold** refer to illustrations.

AUTHORS

GEOFFREY C. HARRISON and **THOMAS F. SCOTT** are educators at the Rumson Country Day School, a K thru 8 school in Rumson, New Jersey. Mr. Harrison is the head of the math department and coordinator of the school's forensics team. Mr. Scott has been teaching upper school history at RCDS for more than 25 years and is head of that department. They enjoy nothing more than a great debate … just ask their students!